Baby Redboots' Revenge

by

[signature]

Philip-Dimitri Galás

illustrations by Jim Nocito

© COPYRIGHT 1993 by Dr. Georgianna Galas
Dimitri Publications
2425 First Avenue
San Diego CA 92101

All rights reserved. Contact Dr. Galas at the above address for permission to perform **Baby Redboots' Revenge**. Due to the unusual nature of the material, it is suggested that the actor view at least one of the videos of Philip-Dimitri Galás' work before performing **Baby Redboots' Revenge**.

First edition, March 15, 1993.

Publisher's Cataloging in Publication

Galás, Philip-Dimitri (1954-1986).
Baby Redboots' Revenge / Philip-Dimitri Galás. —
p.cm.
ISBN 0-9632454-2-2
1. Drama 2. One-act plays 3. Monologues. I. Title.

Table of Contents

The Little Song 1

The Little Speech 3

Baby Four Strings' Manifesto 5

Baby Dimitri's Polka Hell 9

Joe's Get-lost Speech 15

Lament Of The Polka Bass 17

Baby Redboots' Revenge Section 27

Cabaret Poses 35

Singing Poses 37

Dancing Poses 39

Pantomime Poses 41

Circus Poses for Obvious Personalities 43

THE LITTLE SONG

Money ... is burning a hole in my pocket
And liquor is burning a hole in my brain.
Why can't I be like ... a citizen?
Why can't I
Spend just one night being sane?

Why does the darkness seem so attractive?
Why does the sun hurt my eyes?
Goodness ... and faith ... are a real distraction.
I prefer madness and lies.

    (la la la refrain)

Battling boredom became a profession.
We really rolled up our sleeves
Fighting a beast that ... historically speaking
Could never be brought to his knees.
We thought we had him; one night we ... shot him,
Drowned him ... and shot him once more.
Try to imagine our disappointment
When he showed up begging ... for more.

    (la la la refrain)

Philip-Dimitri Galás

THE LITTLE SPEECH

(in darkness)

Every night ... around 11:30,
I get up and walk around the apartment—
At least that's what they tell me downstairs.
Sometimes I hum a little tune—
I don't know how it goes, but they tell me
It's the same one every night.

At some point I start opening drawers ...
and closing drawers ... and opening drawers ... and
closing drawers.
I guess I'm getting dressed.
I take the elevator down
and walk outside and stand in front of our building
just where the light hits me (pause)
and do a little step.
They showed me—it goes like this—

(BABY enters light)

Philip-Dimitri Galás

BABY FOUR STRINGS' MANIFESTO

Bella bella bella bella che bella dancing feet!
I thought I was a flapper in a brandy bath.
I created the cha cha ... om ph ph cum laude.
Daddy said no no no you cannot ... but I did.
Call me a show off and I'll show you—a child star 'twas I.
God's tap dancing ninny—le petittle l'oisea avec rat a tat tat alias Baby Four Strings.
In Europe I went on after the Brothers Lococo and Alice.
I did a little number called
(sings)

>   Too young to love—pitter patter
>   Too young to wait—does it matter?

The authorities were outraged—county to county Daddy came got me ... boarding school was hell ... they never believed I was an attraction abroad ... until one day in church I sang "LINDA AND HER LONDONDERRY AIR ... THEY WERE ALWAYS WELCOME EVERYWHERE."
A fistfight with a nun ensued ... I was flogged in the schoolyard. These are the roots of my pathos.
Why I sing a song
the way I sing a song
is dependent upon your interpretation of the given material, Herr Doktor.
I don't care what Sister Helene Helena Helena Hellena Helena says
YOU CAN'T LOCK UP A TALENT ... DADDY DON'T LET THEM, ET CETERA.

But alas ... alas ...
I was incarcerated ... incarcere ...
It was St. Mary's Bedlam for Baby Dimitri
You've heard the bit about lunatics entertaining the crowned heads. Well, I was a featured performer ...
I **AFFECTED** delusions of grandeur—

> I am the man who invented rubber stamps ... I am Eva Peron ...
> I am Shapera, founder of Shapera invincible old age spot remover ...
> I am Liz Trailer ...
> I am the first scat singer ... bop a du ...
> I am the first torch singer ...
> I am the first chain smoker ...
> I am the
> first dieter ...
> I am the first female impersonator ...
> (Cleopatra was not amused) ...
> I entertained the troops at Balaclava singing "You've Come a Long Way from St. Louis."
> Gertrude Stein confided in me:
> Should I or not should I if not, why then why should I if not then should I then ....

"**GO ON, HONEY,**" I said, and
BOY, DID SHE.

After ten days they released me on my own recognizance and Broadway snapped me up faster than you can say **FREE ASSOCIATION**
It was a revival of "Boomtown Beatnik"
A kinda Romeo and Juliety set in the Industrial Revolution doncha know ... I played Bob, a pocket systems analyst, Garbo played Betsy, a burlesque queen.

Talk about a hit!

       (black out)

Philip-Dimitri Galás

BABY DIMITRI'S POLKA HELL

(for solo performer on bass fiddle)

(bass music playing while Baby Four Strings simulates playing)

(announcement offstage)Good evening, ladies and gentlemen ... now for your dancing pleasure, Oceanside's own Bob Benvenuti & His Polka Chips ... have a good time now and don't forget to Polka with the Bride!

(solo performer/bass fiddle)

Polka polka polka polka polka polka polka till you **puke.**

(sings)
> "In heaven there is no beer
> So drink it all right here
> And when you're gone from here
> Your friends will be drinkin' all your beer"

What key is this guy in anyway? I'm having a chord attack!

Ask, you may
what this has gotta do with being Baby Dimitri—
Famous child star...singing sensation of the traveling stage
I'm asking myself the same thing.
Fact is, my voice changed when I was twenty-five—
It was a fall from grace.

I don't think "The Little Tugboat Song" was intended for a tenor—
And my tap dancing ... well, I was no Ruby Keeler.
I could create an effect, but when it came to holding down a spotlight ... no one ever *warned* me.

Until one day: Sissy Gabon, our fearless band leader, took me aside
>"See that bass fiddle, Baby?
>You and me and that bass fiddle's gonna have a little **TALK**
>About how you might **STARVE** to death!"

Well, God Bless ... God Bless you Sissy Gabon ... but I still can't play this thing
G-D-A-E (plunking strings) B-flat ... is all I know.
The rest is my serious expression ... my God-given sense of time and lots of this (slides hands up and down fingerboard)—
They think I'm really cookin' up here
Not that they can hear a goddamn thing anyway over that screaming accordion—
until **HE** fucks up the tempo, then it's all **MY** fault!

This, for instance, is the foremost spastic
"Beer Barrel Polka" I've ever played in my life.
Look out there—They're all tripping over themselves.
Someone should arrest this man for killing the dead.

Oh oh here it comes ... here it comes
My favorite part of the evening
We're getting excited—"I Got You Under My Skin"
God I despise this song
"So Deep in the Heart / You're Really a **Part** of Me."

Baby Redboots' Revenge

Ezra Pound wrote it, doncha know, in collaboration with Sophie Tucker—
What a team!!! *No please*
please ... **please** ... don't sing it
please don't let that little Napoleon who thinks he's Sinatra sing it ... I'm dying, Egypt, dying ....

If you knew the things I used to do with a song!
And don't think I didn't try and sing for these s.o.b.'s,
But I heard them gossiping—said I sounded like Ellen Forrest—
Very funny
If they'd have seen how I used to break 'em up back east!
Used to build whole numbers around my talent ... put one of the showgirls on as my mother—
running off with a gambler, *leaving the poor Baby Dimitri, alone in his basket, headed downstream singing:*

    (Does "After You've Gone" full tilt, practically
        dropping fiddle—fades/re-poses)

My fingers hurt ... God help me ... this isn't my instrument ....
What's this now?
What's this?
The father of the bride is proposing
something to our fearless band leader
Three bucks each for an extra half hour of music
Oh, this is Hell
In Hell I'll be playing weddings
In Hell I'll be stuck on the bandstand of the V.F.W. of Hell
Playing "The Hawaiian Wedding Song"
WHILE THAT POOR OLD THING down there on

the dance floor in the string tie pretends to conduct us with the **SWIZZLE STICK**

"Awwwww **Hit it boys** ... **C'MON LADS!**"

He wants more **BASS**
Yes sir ... sir yes sir ... sir yes sir
I'll give you more **BASS**

(picks up bass, threatens to throw it/ sudden break in composure/ screech)

... you **OLD AIRCRAFT CARRIER**

You and missy out there smiling,
telling me to smile more ... flashing me the big V (does so).
Oh, next time I bring a gun on the job
40 dollars ain't enough, baby, it ain't enough **YOU POLKAHOLICS**

What? Don't TELL ME THE NEXT SONG IS IN THREE FLATS
WHAT'S THREE FLATS TO ME BUT A BROKEN CAR ...
And those young men looking up at me like I'm some kinda **freak**
They wanna hear the new sound ... Rock and Roll ... Rock and Roll
We play (sing) "Kansas City" real fast to shut 'em up
And they look right at **ME** like I'm from outer space
...
I'm affected, can't ya see I'm not MEANT for this?

Do you know who I am, you brother of the goddam bride?
Do you know that I hate you?
> Like I hate the Shottish
> Like I hate the foxtrot
> Like I hate the samba
> the mamba and the cha cha

Like I hate the **goddamn Polka**
The polka
the polka
The polka is the mangiest idea the human race ever had!

If ever I come into power I will pass **Laws** to prevent public polka-ing
and all polkees and polkettes will be shot on sight
and every accordion
EVEN IN ITALY
confiscated and personally trampled by **me**....

Sincerely Yours,
Baby Dimitri

Philip-Dimitri Galás

JOE'S GET-LOST SPEECH

Alright that's enough, bass fiddle.
Bring the glasses up here.
I have closed twenty minutes.
You clear out or you'll be thumping that cracker barrel
in the drunk tank!
Say ... ain't you gotta wife somewhere?
Go play **her** a lullaby.
She'll tell ya you've got talent ...
no ... I told ya.
I don't know no redboot or baby anything.
Never played here and she never **will**.
I'm getting a big band jukebox in here
with a couple polkas on it,
a couple ballads,
the anniversary waltz,
happy birthday
and "Goodnight Sweetheart."
So I won't have to put up with you
goddamn prima donna musicians anymore!

LAMENT OF THE POLKA BASS

(repeat/percussion) (repeat over and over)

Ladies and gentlemen, don't forget to polka with the bride. Ladies and gentlemen, don't forget to polka with the bride.
Shacklers and fettermen, run the gauntlet, thumbscrews and the rack. Pokers and manacles. Pincers and calipers ...

(pose)

There's the bride up on the catwalk, tipping a vat of hot oil, nails scratching through her veils—Mrs. Attila the Hun's waltzing with her husband in this rented wretched hall. And I, Baby Four Strings, several hours into the battle with his fingers fiddling while nothing burns ... save the bride—unwrapping endless wafflemakers in search of an uncle's extravagance.

"Play it again," booms in my head. The band's raging out of control. The accordionist, Red-In-The-Face, is putting on a show for the talent scouts of his sick fantasy world, incriminating me, Baby Four Strings.

(face in hole of cardboard bass)

It's 2:30 and everybody's gone home except for Joe. I'm here in Joe's rental hall after a four-hour job, playing because I like to. I can't stop the music. How could anyone stop B-flat, A-flat cold-water-flat. One bar, two bar, Joe's bar—that's where I am, watching the ice melt, about to tell you how this is not going to be another rap about performing till your limbs ache, because this is not performing—this is going *thump*, and being invisible until you stop going *thump* and they miss you. This is holding up the bottom going thump and they miss you.

Poor Millie. Waiting at home in front of the television. Will she ever understand my devotion to this ... music? *Used to come and sit at that table,* talk to the wives of the band, all of them 500 years older than she, all of them waiting two hours with *their hands folded before a husband came down* to dance with them. I danced with Millie. *Then Millie* went over to the bar and talked to the lady bartender and was having the time of her life until she said she hated country music. If she'd look over the bar she'd have seen the gal was wearing cowboy boots.

I followed Millie with my eyes. She walked over to one of the vacant tables and sat down, and looked at everybody dancing. The wives of the band were real insulted. Then the whole band got insulted. Especially Elmo, on drums. Mrs. Elmo took him aside during the second break. After that he stopped talking to me and hasn't since ... unless you consider "howdy, yup, sure is" conversation.

Millie swears she did not call Elmo's wife a Big-Nose From Hell. She just said "Mind your own damn business you middle class reactionary old shit for brains."

I can see Millie at home, reaching for the last beer. She'll put it on top of the television and stare at it and dare herself. I'll come in at three-thirty and she'll pretend to be asleep so I won't curse her for taking it.

You wanna hear a secret? We're not even married. We're strangers in town. The neighbors bark all night and the dogs gossip. Sometimes we get so angry we pass out. We eat wrong, too.

(waltz)

In our little love-nest that's dark and dumpy, as corny as neon-flashing, I see Millie in big slippers and me smoking, sitting on the side of the shot mattress with my shirt-sleeves rolled up and my hand in my hair looking like the man who reached the fork in the road and lost his job or got somebody pregnant. Millie's got her arms crossed looking like she *did it to me*. She gazes out the window, then back at me and says, "You sideman ... you ... *thumper!*"

She says I should have saved up for an electric bass and got a job with Elvis or somebody. She thinks my music is ... hokey. I say hokey makes it sound **happy**. It's not happy. It's not even dinner music. It's leftovers music. *Hot plate music.* She says, "Shut up, you dumb bastard, I got the point ... yesterday." She says we should throw ourselves out windows, that all musicians are monkeys and playing music connects us to apes, and they should keep them high up in trees or in cages so people like her can read books in peace and not have to live with men who beat on tables with their fingers and scat-sing every goddamn thing or get challenged by some piece of shit on the radio, or say things like "Chick Singer."

We argue. I say I'm trying, Millie. She says, "You're hooked on American failure, you want all the dark patches to be some black and white movie about drunks with talent who sleep with their clothes on and the wives who put up with it.

"Well, run the credits, monkey, and let's see cartoons again. I want a place to walk around in. Not this *pad*, this splinter ... and that fucking ghost that keeps saying I'm a slut and how I better get the hell out before the captain gets here. As if I know who the fuck the captain is. Would you tell me who the **fuck** the captain is?"

One day I think I'll leave Millie. Or just let her kill me. Between us we've collected enough exotic moments of big city nightlife *at low ebb* to fill a *Police Gazette*. We've committed crimes against culture, where the status quo's a golfer looking to get some off a poor dear who works there, whose boyfriend's doing homework out in the car. The nightmare is her wanting it. The Devil never disappoints a dreamer.

I've seen gals with their best shoes on leading conga lines all around this place. Conga. Conga. Conga. She wears everybody out. Then she comes up to the bandstand and asks if we can play *"To Each His Own"* —her favorite song. The band leader, who hates her, hands her the microphone and starts playing her favorite song as a cha cha cha. She says it's a ballad. He says, "In C-sharp it's a ballad, in F minor seventh it's a **polka** and in about ten seconds

Baby Redboots' Revenge

it's going to be a **march**." She's fleeing in tears when he picks up the mike himself and he sings her favorite song like it's the only song in the world.

You see, these people are barbarians. Nothing to romanticize. It's important that you understand this. They should be lined up. Trap 'em in their big cars and terrorize them. Tell them Millie would like words with them. The door goes bang, someone gets slapped around. I hear Millie saying "Flaxy's the name, Flaxy Four Strings." Someone's pleading. A blast. A zing. Millie's blowing smoke from her pistol. The gun's pointed at me now and Millie's saying "Sing Monkey. Make some sense real quick! You idolize dames and dumb singers—you and those morons who line up to see supper shows about nuns that don't shut up, and female-impersonator, prisoner wrestlers. Let's have it monkey ... PERFORM!"

My bass fiddle sits in the corner like the baddest boy in class. I tap him on the shoulder and he *falls into* my arms. Millie cocks her pistol and waits with her legs akimbo until I sing—something pretentious about how liars make great companions, marrying blondes all over California, reading books full of murder and how it's a big sad world full of small illusions. "I've heard that," she says, and shoots me.

I wake up on a precipice holding my bass fiddle. Burning bodies fall around me. Thump thump isn't that Cleopatra? Thump thump isn't that Mata Hari? Thump thump, it's Millie again, holding out a hoop for clowns to jump through. It's Bimbo and Bumbo with their butts on fire and Millie vocalizing. I'm plucking the cat gut G-string, only the cat's still alive and down there chewing my ankles and saying "Give it back, give it back, give it back," in a midget voice. Elmo and the accordionist float by at a little round table. The accordionist's cigarette isn't *burning* smoke, but little notes everywhere that Elmo keeps catching and eating.

A whole fan club is marching with banners depicting the mediocre singer they adore, *the lovely Baby Redboots*. Her vibrato shatters walls of stained glass that shower down upon her fans. Bloodied, they march through hell for their Baby ... Redboots.

Up above, Millie breaks Baby Redboots' records with her bare hands. She's saying, "I thought she always sounded like a tugboat horn pretending to be British. Or an air-raid warning for flying monkeys. Or a sing-along dot that jumped off the song into somebody's knickers. Oh never mind. Oh never mind. Oh never mind. Oh never mind.

(slow)

I'm thumping and the cat's got a tiger's head on it, and Millie's campaigning against singers in general and Joe's closing the place, telling me to take my big guitar and beat it. I want to say fuck you all, but they've got me by the short hairs. I could be a bum in a second and they know it—hock this big sling-shot for a month of six-packs and wind up with Millie's hand caught up in my hair, lifting me up to look at every half hour like there's a clock in my face.

(slow)

I'm not waking up, the tongues hanging out. In a dream I say, "And-a-one and-a-two and-a-three and-a-four and-a-one and-a-two and-a-three and-a-four and-a ..."

(slow)

I'm conducting a canyon like *it's* a swing band. Grow trees, grow! Look at the donkey going down down down down and the sun going up. More rock. More Indian arrowheads and a nudist camp. Somebody playing bass fiddle for nude dancing.

I sit up in bed and Millie looks at me. She *sticks* a cigarette in my mouth and lights it and tells me to cut it out. Cut what out? I'll cut my heart out and say happy birthday, Millie.

She says, "Anyone who plays 'Apple Blossom Time' more than fifty times automatically goes insane. There's a study to prove it." She's watched me become a lunatic before I had time to get with the beat of my own generation. What a tragedy. She's part of it. She hates me for it.

(pause)

Joe's going to call the police and have me dragged out. I tell him the boys left without me, and I've got to carry my bass fiddle home twenty blocks in the fog because the bastard won't fit in a cab.

(shout)

I'm out on the street in the fog with the red light flashing. Up in our building there's only one light on—the television. I see Millie's silhouette against the white wall, still as can be. Smoke is the only thing moving up there. I want to call up, "HEY LADY, THAT'S ONE GRUESOME SIGHT," but she beats me to it.

Hands on hips in the window—my Millie. For one moment of recognition, we're Romeo and Juliet. Then she remembers.

I stuff my hands down in my pockets and pull out what I didn't drink of tonight's wages and hold it up like an offering.

Millie throws open the window and screams for the world to hear: "**I don't want you to give me the shirt off your back, I don't want my old shirt back!**"

There's a rumbling. White convertibles with little girls at the wheel, driving standing up like water skiers, wave to Millie as they circle out in the middle of the lake of empty lanes—running me down again, running me down again, running me down again.

Millie's applauding—a standing ovation in the loveless window. I watch as the slivers and chips of my darling bass fiddle form little crucifixes in midair and come raining slowly down upon me. Me. Me, the Baby Four Strings: Bossing nothing around in the world of music. Bossing nothing around in the world of women.

(advances wide-eyed with these lines—
expectation)

Bossing nothing around but my own shadow, that
keeps snapping its fingers, in spite of me.

Philip-Dimitri Galás

BABY REDBOOTS' REVENGE SECTION

(snapping fingers)

Let's pretend I'm in the middle of my life. Dead center.

(hands raised)

Nothing moving from the East. Nothing moving from the left. Miraculously, I have lost interest in performing.

(lyrically)

Let's jus' pretend.
I'm the poet who's lost his love of language.
I need wine to rhyme.
Give me a rope to skip.
Let's say I'm bored to death up here. Let's jus' pretend.

Any second I'm going to drop the Baby from my name and consider moving to the outlying areas. I'm about to be overheard saying:

(all one pose)

Just give me a porch, a rockin' chair, two hounds, stick a pipe in my mouth and I'll just sit there with my winchester 'cross my lap and listen to the ants ... farm.

(mime seated)

Philip-Dimitri Galás

The competition would *like* to think I'd give up that easily. Somewhere out in space, in a motel in Southern California is Baby Redboots, a malignant memory, my old, old partner. She's flipping switches out there, trying to brain-wave me into mediocrity, trying to make me quit show business.

(aside)

She's a whole trailer-camp rolled into one woman. She's telephoning Millie. She tracked us down and warned us to keep out of her way.

(to audience)

Millie didn't need any more encouragement to leave me.
Now they're probably holed up together slugging a wall and cursing a television, wondering how they put up with that uppity Baby Bastard all those years.

Well, those weird sisters aren't dogging me around any more.
My eyes are still full of Paradise.
Palm trees fluttering around a black moon—can't you see it?

(voice) (slow)

Here's what happened, ladies and gentlemen—Baby Red Boots put a **whammy** on me.
A little doll clutching a little bass fiddle sits among the lingerie full-a-*pins*.
Big pins, small pins, hat pins, tacks, needles—her hatred is indiscriminate.
And you know what?

And you know what? Her vaudeville curse worked on me ....

One day I was slicking my hair back.
I had a handful of photographs of me at my best.
I was prepared to sell anything on camera.

    (pointing to parts of body) (lowers body)

Then it hit me—right here, then here—Right here, then here, then here ...
A little *tune* went through my head.
One we used to sing together.

    (narrative ... to rise agonized)

That wicked witch appeared in my bathroom mirror.
I covered her with shaving cream.
Her face hovered in the white foam. She cackled, I shaved her.
She sang "Harvest Moon" with that little sixteenth note at the end of the moon ... that used to bug me.

    (tired)

I collapsed.
I was hours late for my big appointment listening to myself admit how I'd lost the vitality commonly associated with ... youth
... the **whammy** was on.
Life presented only two ideas—kill yourself or survive.
Living never entered my mind. Baby Redboots called me from her cannibal pot
Go on, Baby, Go on. Try and be wonderful ... just you try!

(fade)

That voice led me down a concrete garden path.
It said audition for movie. I did. No luck.
I auditioned for musicals. I did. No luck.
I auditioned for chorus lines. I did. No luck.
I auditioned for circuses. No luck.
I auditioned for lounge acts. No luck.
I auditioned for Shopping Center Santa Claus. No luck. No luck.
I auditioned for the Salvation Army Band. No luck.
Her **whammy** had me by the tap shoes.

Buffaloing off to shuffalo.
Beginning no Beguine.
I called Millie for help.
She read me passages from the Bible. In German.
It was unbearable.
I looked at a bottle and the bottle looked back at me.
Sometimes it poured me a drink—when it wasn't dancing on the mantlepiece or hopscotching across the checkered kitchen tablecloth.

(bent down)

I had to see the Gypsy.
I had to see her.
"Gypsy," I said, "Do something."
Gypsy looked into her crystal.
And had a good laugh
and said:

"You ... the Baby Four Strings ... shunned by Venus and blacklisted by Apollo himself ... your problem is ... you ... are ... avant ... avant ... avant-garde. God help you, how unfortunate!"

"So what do I do, **Gypsy**? What do I do?"
Well, Gypsy come to find out, had done her time in Art School and made a small fortune in New York counseling art students (hand on hip) predicting massive grants and sales to corporations of aborted fingerpaintings of idiotic haircuts posing as people pretending they don't know how to paint.

"Listen," she said, "put together an act and write a mean press release."
She gazed into her crystal ball and read that press release:

(Gypsy voice ... fast ...)

"**Hipper than trans-modernism, cornier than science, mainstream of pop iconoclasm, pastiche, done-to-death desublimation. Gimme a one two three, Baby's gonna shatter his own myth and perform as somebody else entirely. Lights, music ... here we have a veritable sociologist ... elevating the gesture of grabbing a microphone from self-promotion to the survival instinct.**"

"Thank you, Gypsy," I said. "Thank you, thank you thank you.

"**Shut up**, and get on with it," she said, "I know these red boot types."

The only way to break their curse is to stand in front of an audience in a small theater somewhere in Hollywood, only a breath away from the gates of ... Paramount.
Stand like Swanson in the ruins of the Roxy.

(does)

And tell them just what you think of anyone who performs.
Or thinks of performing

>   (Swanson face) (also Swanson voice)

Get a chair and stand on it.

>   (pause on chair—Swanson pose)

And just when you're about to sing your little song, (on chair) stop yourself and say ...

>   **Ladies and gentlemen, allow me to demonstrate every possible performance pose. Anyone who pretends that his range goes beyond the following is a goddamn liar.**
>   **We all function neatly within the parameters**

of these vulgarities.

>   (shouts)

Take this, Baby Redboots!
Take this, Millie!

CABARET POSES

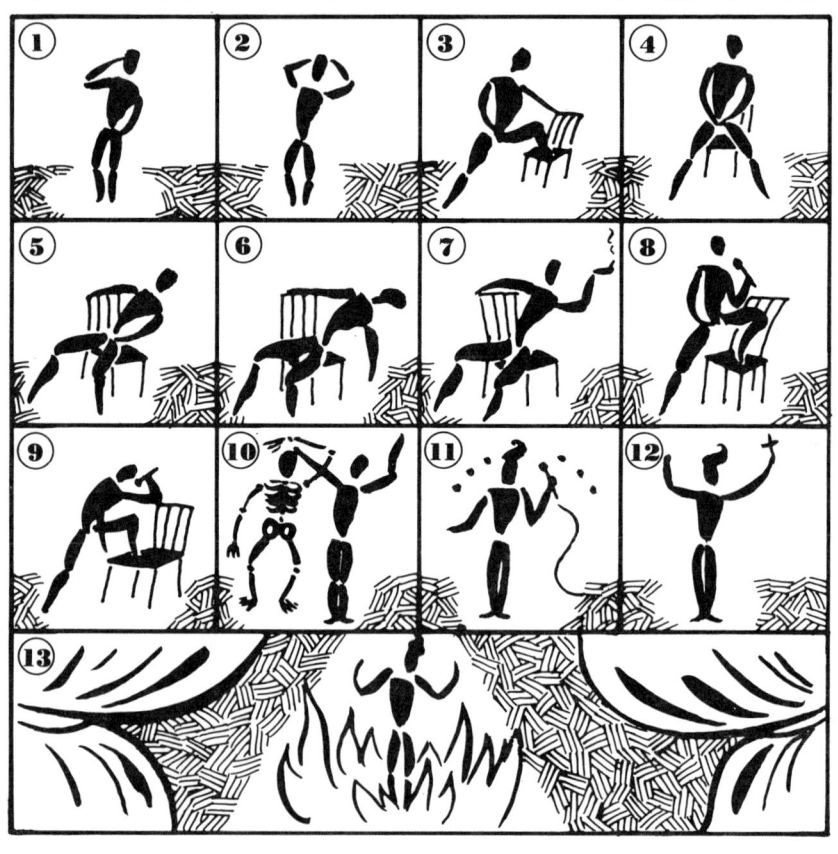

CABARET POSES

Pose One: **Cabaret Poses**

(poses proceed with the chair)

Contemplating moral abandon.
Conceptualizing moral abandon.
Experimenting with moral abandon.
Actually feeling **driven** to moral abandon.
Actual moral abandon.
Recovering from actual moral abandon.
Making a lifestyle out of moral abandon.
Singing about moral abandon.
Singing about moral abandon night after night after night after night.
Abandoning moral abandon in favor of cheap theatrics.

(get skeleton) (skeleton thrown to stage)

Going to Las Vegas.
Going Christian.
Going to Hell, anyway.

Philip-Dimitri Galás

SINGING POSES

(skeleton in front of him)

Church singing.
Opera singing.
Show singing.
Jazz singing.
Pop singing.
Rock singing.
Country singing.
Torch singing.
Lounge singing.
Lousy singing.
Singing the national anthem.
Singing for company.
Singing in the rain.
Singing in the shower.
Singing for your dinner.
Singing like Dinah Washington.
Lip synching.
Not singing ... daring anyone else to sing.

Philip-Dimitri Galás

DANCING POSES

On toe.
Off toe.
Shuffle-ball-change.
Taking inspiration from ethnic dance.
The can can/the cha cha.
Shuffle-ball-change.
Dancing on someone's grave
A rain dance.
A song and dance.
Pretending to have fun dancing.
Telling yourself Isadora Duncan got away with murder and inventing a vicious comic sketch called "Isadora in Pasadena."

    Act 1. Isadora extolling the microwave.
    2. Isadora scolding the television.
    3. Isadora marvelling at formica.
    4. Isadora insisting on Congoleum.
    5. Isadora discovering the cassette.
    6. Isadora taking power steering for granted.
    7. Isadora snipping coupons, tragically.

Tap dancing so fast they can't even tell that your goddamn feet are moving.
Dancing just to show off your legs.
Modern dance.
Post modern dance.
Post mortem dance.

    (Directly into next section)

Philip-Dimitri Galás

PANTOMIME POSES

Walking.
Window washing.
Pulling the rope.
Flying the kite.
Picking the rose.
Smelling the rose.
Climbing the ladder.
Falling off.
Walking.
Window washing.
Pulling the rope.
Roping the pull.
Kiting the fly.
Rosing the pick.
Smelling the ladder.
Walking the rose.
Flying the window.
Rosing the rope.
Pulling the smell.
Deciding to speak.
Speaking.
Deciding to stop flying the kite.

Philip-Dimitri Galás

CIRCUS POSES FOR OBVIOUS PERSONALITIES

(fast)
Sawing a lady in half ... tight rope ... jump rope ... bondage
Chain-smoking in your trailer.
Considering another career in burlesque.
Using your G-string as a sling shot.
Commiserating with the parasitic twin.
Having breakfast with the tattooed lady.
Shrieking as the aerialist falls to her death.
Blaming Coco the Clown for cutting the wire.
Being pursued by Coco the Clown through a maze of trailers.
Defending yourself with an axe.
Driving through small towns in a stolen car as the radio screams ... **"Beloved Coco the Clown found slain!"**
Hiding from justice by opening in a club in San Diego and desperately improvising a little song that's going to save you from life under the curse of **Baby Redboots** ....

Which means getting back on the chair ... and standing on it.
As the authorities wait and smoke at the stage door in their Hawaiian shirts, you kill time like Scheherazade ... in fact, you make a whole profession out of it ... you begin: Ladies and uh ... gentlemen (direct to house—non parenthetical),

Philip-Dimitri Galás

a little song from the archives of avant-vaudeville ...
(looking about/fast)
Whatever became of Morgan Morgan?
Whatever became of Happy? (big smile)
Whatever became of the pretentious boy?
Who sang Carmen on the trapeze? ... uh uh uh.
(desperately)
My swan of a heart, ladies and gentlemen ...
Memories of a season
in a circus in Hell
Carnival dancers named ... Mabel
My swan of a ...

> Shut up memory
> Shut up past
> Pull down the big top
> I'm getting truss slavely just thinking
> about the future of my past

Uh Uh Uh ...

> Whatever became of Darla Furlough
> And all those Russian Ponies
> We had coffee in Minneapolis
> Between breakdowns ... Oh God, help me!

Whatever became of ... whatever became of ...

> I'm gonna finish this song if it kills you
> Baby Redboots. I'm gonna shake you for
> good ... I'll have my own act if I have to
> bump and grind on your tombstone with
> my jockstrap full of dollar bills.

(bravely)
Whatever became of Icarus Mahoney, Tightrope walker extraordinaire.
Bet the State of California he could stretch ...

dental floss from Lake Shasta to Tijuana and coast down it on ice skates with a cigar smoking, sarcastic son of a bitch of a monkey on his head ... he got as far as Capistrano, where the swallows attacked the monkey and ...
Whatever became of ...
Whatever became of ...
Whatever became of ...Mavis Davis?

   300 pounds of the Blues

   (poignantly)

   And not enough common sense
   in all that woman for a little girl

Whatever became of ...
Hell, this one's easy ...
Parchesi, the clown
who jumped into the great Canal at Corinth—
One mile down into the emerald waters.
He went splash and was never seen again. The Greeks loved it. Whatever became of that stand-up comedian who ran out of material so did an act about his mother, dragged that poor woman through hell in search of a good laugh. When the fable of her chicken soup didn't get them going, he decided to give up the human touch. He had his mother bringing in strange men at stranger hours for the chicken soup. The audience liked that. So he decided to go even further and make his mother into a drunkard—this round decent woman who barely spoke English—he made her reckless.The audience wanted more. From then on out everything became blah blah blah, my Mother the Messalina of population 500 and her endless

45

supply of Wild Turkey and the military coming and going. When the comedian hit TV his mother pulled the shades in her little house and hasn't opened them since. Stand-up comedians should be locked in trunks with starving wolverines ... (pause) Where was I?

My swan of a heart ... my swan of a ...

Whatever became of Prussia, the belly dancer who took up with the half-man/half-woman named China and bore two ...ow ... children, Pete and Dinah, who became teenage hellcats in mohawks and tattooed their parents while they slept. Prussia's circus friends tried to help. The fat lady kept ... ow ... kept ... kept saying Switzerland, Switzerland, Switzerland. But she was wrong wrong wrong. Switzerland was ow tedious. Prussia was mocked. China, deported and Pete and Dinah were executed.

Ow! (pause) I'm depressed! I'm depressed, ladies and gentlemen. Gypsy you lied to me, Gypsy, you charlatan. I just felt another pin go in my swan of a heart.
It's not working.
I'm singing my swan of a butt off
Because ... ow ow ow beloved Baby Redboots wants me to throw my hands up and say yes yes I'll play bass fiddle on a rowboat cruise down Niagara ... but I won't play bass fiddle ever again ever ever ever ever ever ...
OWWWWWWWW

What the **Hell** ever became of Mademoiselle Arlotte
    (tone shift)
Ringmistress of the chateau de Petite Betes Flea Circus.
Bade me peer through her magnifying glass.
There, on top of a letter opener—fifteen fleas:
Jacques, Jacques, Jacques, Jacques, Jacques,
Alphonse, Pierre, Pierre, Pierre, Pierre,
Yvette, Babette, Mistinguette, and I forget.
All elaborately dressed and re-enacting Cleopatra's entrance to Rome. "There goes the young Caesar," she would always say and applaud so loudly she'd kill most of them.
Oh, it didn't matter. She liked starting from scratch.
    (breaks into "After You Are Gone" ...
    breaks down)
Ow ... you old vixen (grabbing groin) Not there! Not there!
I don't mind the pain. I just don't want anyone thinking this is a celebration of castration anxiety, or a soap opera audition. I already did my time on stage being Southern ... with my Sleeveless-Terrorizing of the lovesick and neurotic. I smoked Chesterfields in cluttered rooms under a ceiling fan. I screamed **Bella hey Bella.**
When boundless masculine energy became unfashionable,
I cheered loudly ... and I **sang** ...
(sings: Bananas [X8] ... Coffee [X4] double time)
    (softly)
My Swan of a heart
    (big pose)

(loudly)
Whatever ... became ... of Anabella ...Notorious groupie.
Used to pursue One-Man Bands around the country.
Stood there batting her lashes while they honked and pounded in shopping centers all over America.
That's how she began her dancing career.
The crowd needed more than a man with four saxophones in his mouth.
She knew they did ... they needed ... exotic dancing. She was sure they did.
Anabella shimmied so hard they had to call the cops. And one after another, the one-man bands abandoned her in roadside diners everywhere.
They said they were going to the bathroom.
She'd fly outside, still holding her coffee cup and watch the dust settle as the one-man band van made it's way to the freeway. She shuffled back into the diner and, if it was real late, tell the waitress the whole sad story.
She'd break every heart in the house, and when the diner closed they'd take her out and buy her drinks and everything would be lovely until someone put Elvis on the jukebox, then Anabella would mount the nearest table and make an appalling spectacle of herself ... stripping through her tears ... sobbing her way to felony in a country too young for her talent ...
(evangelical/transformed)
Ah wait wait wait ... wait wait wait ...
(feeling body/voodoo stab points)
Is the pain off? I think the pain's off ladies and gentlemen. Did I say something right?

Baby Redboots' Revenge

        (hushing with index finger to lips)
Shhhhhhh ... listen ... you hear that ... a little song....
                (singing)
           Baby Redboots is my darling
           Baby Redboots is my love

           She's the only four foot manna
(softly)   That I'm thinking of
           And my heart goes wiki wiki
           And my knees go wicky du
           And my swan-of-a-heart gets kinda bitsy kinda ... kinda
        (stops/shocked/possessed voice)
Aye gotta fake into the part yeah yeah wha wha wha!
So then why doncha just come on over here and take some Ha ha see whaddaya got ... ba ba ba **Baby**
    (Waving finger as Baby Redboots—playing two parts)

        (all evil Baby voices)

        REDBOOTS
That's not nice. That's not nice.
        FOUR STRINGS
I'll show you **nice**, you little prima donna.
        REDBOOTS
Now, you know, dear Four Strings, that the dance goes:
KICK KICK KISS
KICK KISS KICK

KISS KISS KISS KISS KISS
KICK KISS KICK
          FOUR STRINGS
Like hail it do. You ... red ... boot ... it goes:
KICK TRIP KICK
BOOT KICK THUD
STOMP KICK STOMP KICK
BANG-A-LANG BUMP!
          REDBOOTS
No! No! Help me, Mr. Ziegfield, he's **hurting me!**
          FOUR STRINGS
In my dreams you're shark bait!
    (looks up, as if taking audience request, manic
          smile)
What? Ventriloquism?
You want ventriloquism?
Aw-right, lovely ... my infinite variety ...
          (angrily/English accents)
My dummy, Garhoolicabritches, had an accident. (rattling wood) Fell down lotsa stairs, but insisted on coming tonight, ladies and gentlemen.
So, Garhoolica, what makes you such a trooper?
          (rattling wood response)
Oh, is that so? How 'bout a transfusion of Elmer's Glue?
          (rattling wood)
Don't tell me, you used to be a bass fiddle.
Committed suicide when the Viola ran off with the Cello.
Take this.
          (transfusion)
There, you like that ... Get you back on the beam, so to speak.
          (rattling wood)

Baby Redboots' Revenge

He says in his next life he wants to come back as a billy club and beat the living hell out of the audience. Now is that nice, Garhoolica, is that nice?
        (rattling wood)
He says he hasn't had sex in five months 'cause I won't let him near a toy store.
        (matter of factly to dummy)
Now, **Listen to me**, you son of a birch, (lower voice)

I'll show you what it's like to have an evil eye trained on you,
trying to constrict your swan of a heart.
Turns a spotlight into a flame thrower.
        Before you know it you want to stay home.
        You don't wanna sing your little song anymore.
        You want to squeeze the vibrato right out of your voice
        And bind your feet and write criticism.
        Make a profession out of enjoying nothing,
        Except in your dreams when you extend one hand to put the horns up, and hold that microphone to your lips and growl and say:
        I got rrrrrrrockets in my pppppppockets;
        I got rrrrrrockets in my head;
        I can shake I can rrrattle;
        I can roll over dead.
        (sings)
You know, ladies and gentlemen,
I was dancing with Medusa
to the Tennessee Waltz
        (back to talking)

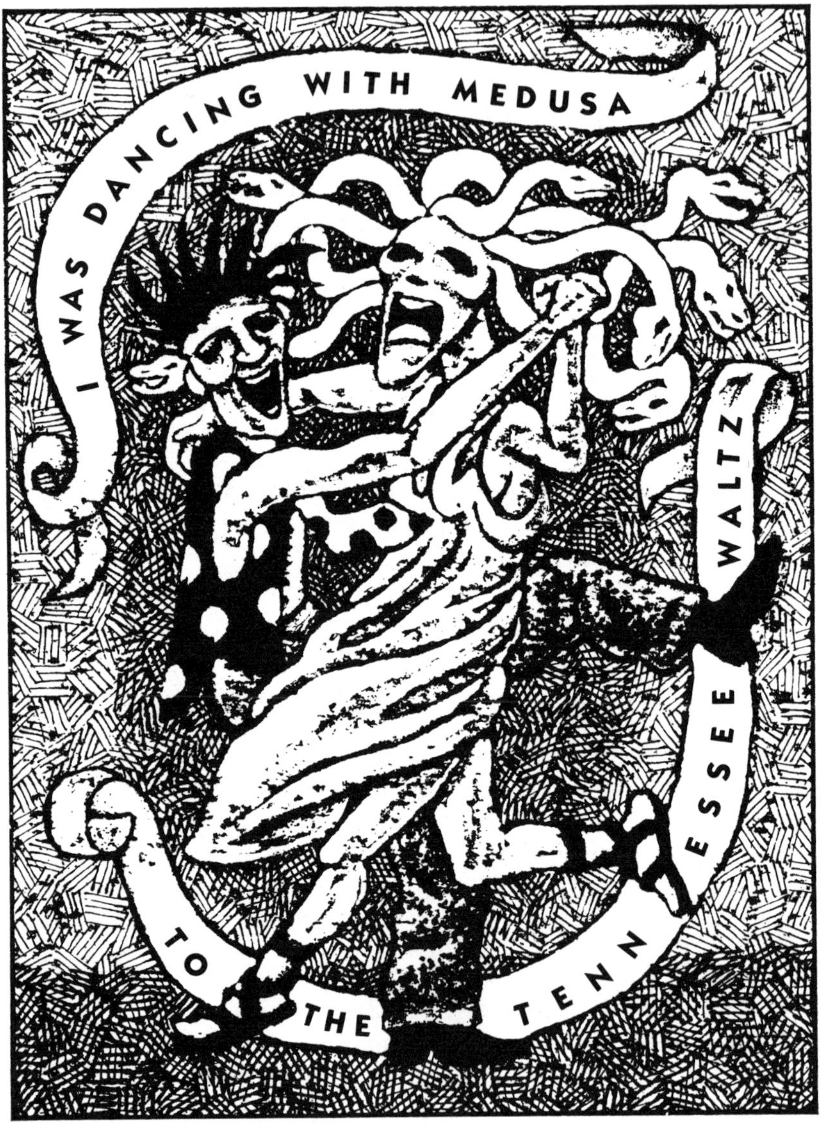
I WAS DANCING WITH MEDUSA
TO THE TENNESSEE WALTZ

when something peculiar occurred to me.
I am a Cyclops in love with a Gorgon.
Our parents are scandalized anyway, so what have we got to lose?
It was telepathy—we both started singing:
> With a raw tye tippy
> With a raw tye oh
> with a raw tye tippy tippy
> raw tye oh!

Boy what fools we were, ladies and gentlemen, missing our golden opportunity because we were so afraid that some ... some ... red bastard was going to tell us mythological references were irrelevant and art could live without them.
We both knew, Medusa and I, that there was nothing more irrelevant that working class heroes.
Why have working class heroes when you can have Working Class ... God Build Statues—show a lotta Mussolini.
Congress could tell that nothing inspires a nation like perfect buttocks. Which ... immediately ... disqualifies a certain red boot I know of,
Whom ... I place in the general category of truculent chanteuses.
Another one of these song-stresses who get their past read and tell the nation that in another life they were Queen Block-That-Kick of Egypt? Why is it always Egypt? Always the same queen. I tell you, 5,000 women went to the same swami who's driving a Rolls through Beverly Hills drinking holy water out of a blonde's deck shoe on his way to tell the latest Tiddy Winks Champion of Tinsel Town how she, too, was

Queen Block-That-Kick ... in another life.
And I'll be goddamned if I'll languish in obscurity with my swan of a heart as they cackle out three notes, get (screaming) famous and are still not happy because they wanna take responsibility for the pyramids ... they wanna take responsibility for ... the ... sand ...
Doncha, Redboots?
Doncha, Redboots?
You fuckin' red boot.
You ... defective thespian,
Superannuated sideshow puta

> Thump goes my Swan of a Heart
> Thump, ladies and gentlemen
> My swan of a heart,
> Ladies and gentlemen

My swan of a heart ... lost on a river of *SHIT!*
I stood before my public and screamed until that voodoo sweat bled through my duckling feathers.
What an ugly image ... but what a blessed event. This exorcism ... backstage grease pencils leapt out of make-up kits and wrote profanities about me all over the mirrors.
The audience roared.
And I knew then it wasn't enough to shake the curse of Baby Redboots.
I had to ... return the favor.
I didn't need the gypsy for this recipe.
I used common sense: and on a bonfire made out of bass fiddles
I got sequins from a singer's cocktail dress,
Marabou from a showgirl's feather boa;
Stirred in lotsa vodka

Baby Redboots' Revenge

with a big band leader's baton,
got a strippers blessing and **voila,
a curse on those red boots.**

She got on stage. It was a big revival ... New York City ... Associated Press ... Vaudeville stars from the world over. She was going to show them everything she knew about performing—from Shakespeare to the shimmy.
She was prepared to upstage everybody and make the event ... hers.
But ....
She sat down at the piano, but she couldn't see her fingers anymore.
The love sonnets she recited turned into pornography. She could not stop speaking pornography.
She was halfway through a scene from "St. Joan," when her mouth started singing "Too Darned Hot ... It's Too Darned Hot."
She was modeling her old showgirl gowns when it occurred to her that snaps and zippers and tassels defied Jesus, and she stood there and told them why.
She tried to cover up by smiling a lot and showing a lot of cute red boot ...
The audience began cursing, throwing their own cute boots,
Throwing their hats and wigs—anything they could get their hands on.
Baby Redboots wailed, "**Harvest Moon** ... moon ... moon ... moon ... moon ... moon ... moon ...."
And I was in my own dressing room at the time at Radio City Music Hall, and I was watching the

55

whole thing in my mirror. Baby Redboots
throwing herself into the orchestra pit.
  (softly)
Watching her—impale herself on a bass fiddle
bow. A little twitch, a little smile, a little kick kiss
kick and she was ... Dead dead dead dead dead
dead dead dead.
And I stood up.
And for once ...
And for once ...
I sang ... my little song ...
My lovely lovely lovely little song.
All the way through ... completely. And it went
like this:
  (snaps)

  (to black)

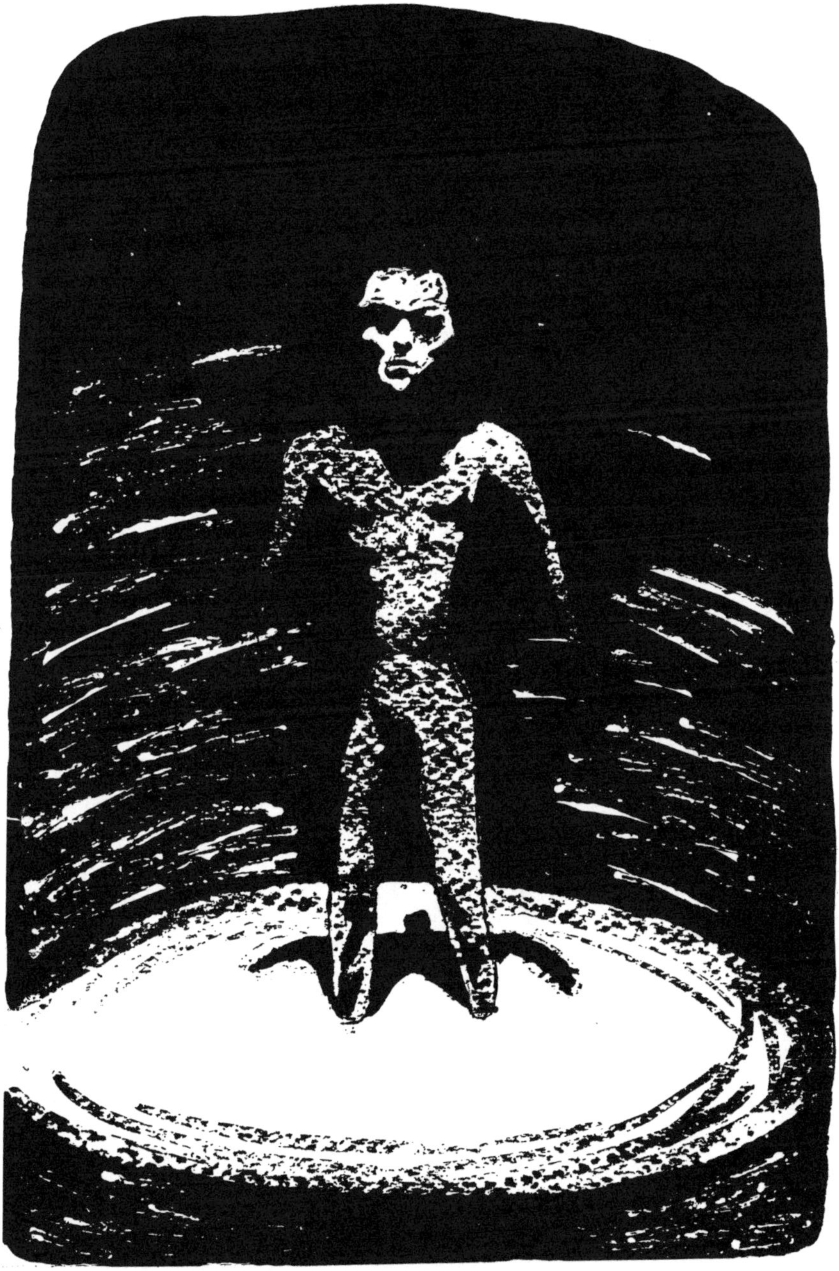

Baby Redboots' Revenge

Philip-Dimitri Galás wrote and performed actively in the U.S. and abroad from 1971 to 1986. He was especially influenced while touring with a company of British circus performers in London and Sweden. He created Avant-Vaudeville, which he called "the only performance style to originate in San Diego." His plays and "avant-vaudevilles" include **"Performance Hell"** for which he received a Hollywood Drama-Logue Award for play-writing, and **"Mona Rogers in Person."**

The extended Los Angeles engagement of **"Baby Redboots' Revenge"** in the spring of 1986 earned Galás an L.A. Weekly Theatre Award and a Hollywood Drama-Logue Award for play-writing. **Jim Nocito**, the illustrator of this script, was the set designer for **"Baby Redboots' Revenge."** *Exoticards*, created by Galás, are known internationally for reviving interest in the cover art of pulp magazines from the 1950's. Philip-Dimitri Galás' untimely demise in 1986 was a tragic loss to the performing and literary arts.

Paperback books by Philip-Dimitri Galás may be ordered with a credit card by calling 1-800/356-9315, or by mail by sending check or money order for the price of the book plus $2.00 shipping and handling for the first title and $.50 for each additional title. California residents, please add sales tax. Wholesale inquiries are welcome. This page may be photocopied for purposes of ordering.

Cigarette Waltz, Seventeen Short Stories Adaptable for Theater
224 pp. . . . . .0-9632454-0-6 . . .$11.95

Avant Vaudeville video $19.95
Due to the unusual nature of the material, it is suggested that the actor view at least one of the videos of Philip-Dimitri Galás' work before performing **Baby Redboots' Revenge**.

Baby Redboots' Revenge, one-man one act
64 pp. . . . . . .0-9632454-2-2 . . . $6.95

Mona Rogers In Person, one-woman one act
96 pp. . . . . . .0-9632454-1-4 . . . $9.95

Send a photocopy of this page with check or money order to:
Dimitri Publications
2425 First Avenue
San Diego CA 92101
Send for a free catalog of Galás' Exoticards and the latest titles from Dimitri Publications!